Ten Reasons Black Folk Should Love Donald Trump

Johnny (Big) Dawgs

© 2020 Johnny (Big) Dawgs

10 Reasons Black Folk Should Love Donald Trump

Unless otherwise identified, Scripture quotations are from the HOLY BIBLE, NEW INTERNATIONAL VERSION ®, Copyright © 173, 178, 194 by International Bible Society Used by permission of Zondervan Publishing House. All rights reserved. Scripture quotations identified KJV are from the King James Version of the Bible.

All rights reserved. No part of this publication may be reproduced, stored in a retrieval system, or transmitted in any form or by any means -- electronic, mechanical, photocopying, recording, or otherwise -- without the prior written permission of author or publisher.

Published by Harrod
Publishing
Printed in the United States
Library of Congress

---

10 Reasons Black Folk Should Love Donald Trump

| Johnny (Big) Dawgs | ISBN: 978-0-9997275-4-6 |

Index

	Preface		
Chapter 1	Barack Obama Humiliated Him at the Correspondents' Dinner	Page 1	
Chapter 2	He Hated John McCain, He Hated John McCain	Page 5	
Chapter 3	He's the Poster Child for the Me-Too Movement	Page 9	
Chapter 4	He Woke Up All the Black Folks to Their (So-Called) Racist Friends	Page 12	
Chapter 5	He Doesn't Tell the Truth and Has Good Lawyers	Page 17	
Chapter 6	He Showed Black Folks How Much Their Votes Really Cares	Page 20	
Chapter 7	He Made Black Folks Engage in the Political Process more	Page 23	
Chapter 8	He Showed Black Folks Who the Real Uncle Toms and Stephens (*Django*) Were	Page 29	
Chapter 9	He Showed Black Folks What Fake Christians and the Real Anti-Christ Looks Like	Page 34	
Chapter 10	White Privilege	Page 38	
	Epilogue	Page 43	
	Voters' Guide	Page 61	
	The Big Finish (Let's Summarize)	Page 90	
	About The Author	Page 97	

Preface

I wrote these definitions down so everybody can get an understanding of what is happening in society, especially in the political arena. Sometimes we read and hear things that we either love or hate simply because of who is saying it. The deliverer of the information cannot simply make it truth or facts, actuality determines that.

Facts – Something that exists – Real – an actual occurrence

Hyperbole – Exaggeration, embellishment, overstatement

Platitudes- A remark in a speech that is overused and has no originality (cliché)

Innuendo – An oblique allusion

Disingenuous – Lacking in honesty, giving a false appearance of simple frankness

Truth – The body of real things, events, and fads; activity

Lies – Distortions, leaving out relevant info, a false statement made with deliberate intent to deceive

Speculation – The forming of a theory or conjecture without firm evidence

Fake – Not Genuine, counterfeit

Bullshitter - (Vulgar) – Someone who lies or exaggerates a lot, especially in order to get noticed.

Fake News – A form of news consisting of deliberate misinformation or hoaxes spread via traditional news media (print or broadcast) or social media.

Good day, good people. Thank you in advance for purchasing this book. In the following chapters we will layout a series of facts and truths that some people will not like, but that is okay. I was told as a young man "just because you don't like the truth it doesn't stop it from being the truth." I had a friend who would always tell me that the truth needs no support and she was absolutely right, it doesn't. It's actuality. I am always stunned when I hear people say that their belief is in science. Science is not a belief, it is actuality! On the other hand, some people will try to use religion as a shield to justify their ignorance. I am a believer in Jesus Christ, and yet boldly stand on the fact that science is real. If anything, it more than justifies the existence of God; but that's a whole different book. In the next 10+ chapters we will explore the facts associated with Mr. Trump. At times when we entertain assumptions, we will be very clear about it. The first assumption we will discuss is that Mr. Trump hates Barack Obama. I say that because of all the times he spends disparaging him and his name, but even that is still an assumption. It's not like Former President Obama battles with him on Twitter or thru the media, nevertheless, Trump attempts to damage his name and legacy at every turn. Still, this is just an assumption, *and yet here we are*! Is this a term that has become so prevalent in the society today? Yep!

"And yet here we are", is used to confirm the obvious of what is happening in now time, especially when it may not be what we wanted or expected to happen. Usually, it has happened after somebody else's prediction to the contrary. For instance, you know when we tell somebody not to give the baby any money because she will put it in her mouth. They insist the baby is going to be okay because they are going to watch her. Time elapses and you see her with the money in her mouth, she comes down with an infection, and you end up in the emergency room. When that same someone insists that they didn't believe the baby would get sick you simply look up and say, "Yet here we are!"

The same principle applies when we hear things like we live in a post racial society, Trump just speaks the truth, racism is a thing of the past, and police are just doing their jobs. However, we all live in a world where the complete opposite exists. My thought is, if a man is assaulted because of the color of his skin, someone would probably suggest that just because the assailant engages with white nationalist propaganda that does not mean racism had anything to do with the assault, yet, the victim is in critical care and the country is more divided than before. Yet here we are! We spend more time than a little bit arguing semantics and not dealing with facts and solutions. People of color suffer more police brutalities than any other race in America. That's a fact! The conversation shouldn't be centered on whether or not this man tried to sell cigarettes as singles or whether or not the police used an outlawed choke hold to kill him. I always say, whoever has the best lawyer wins. Justice may not prevail but money will. I remember watching Elizabeth Warren completely tear apart the CEO of Wells Fargo bank for their unethical business practices. At one point they were forcing bank tellers to steal the identity of their customers, and forge signatures on applications while the institution itself was stealing millions of dollars in over draft fees from the same innocent customers. Interestingly enough, Wells

Fargo would prosecute tellers for stealing a handful of twenties but company executives were stealing millions from unsuspecting consumers and employees. They, the company executives, had money and good lawyers. We always get caught up in the small stuff instead of dealing with the problem and finding the real solutions.

So, we all have heard the many racial things about Donald Trump:

- Discrimination lawsuits
- Birther conspiracy
- Housing discrimination
- Central Park Five
- Black people being dumb

It seems that we ignored the obvious because he has black people such as) Russell Simmons, Shaquille O'Neil, Kanye West, and Ben Carson – so we thought- all around him. Well, the rappers wanted to be caked up like him (not really though-right?). Black folks gave him a pass; it didn't matter that he had confirmed racist contributors in his inner circle (check Stephen Miller). Shaq said Trump was alright – Right? Steve Harvey went to see him, and so did Ray Lewis. I mean those guys are okay. I mean Russell Simmons use to stay at his house. Don King even took him to a church and introduced him. He has a number of black people that will vouch for him so he can't be all that bad. The next line would surely be, "I have plenty of black friends", but isn't that what racist people say when they want others to believe they are not racist!"

I am always amused by the Black and Brown people who stand behind him, waving flags, wearing MAGA hats, smiling I am sure they don't know that if Donald Trump, Stephen Miller, and Steve Bannon had their way, they would be shipped out of this country. It's like they have black people Stockholm syndrome. Let's not forget Stephen was Calvin Candy's man in *Django,* but he was still his slave, and if he would have stepped out of line, he would be given a one-way ticket to nigger heaven by way of hungry dogs. In *Mandingo*, Mead was still a slave as was Blim in *12 Years a Slave*. These are just examples of how no matter what kind of trinkets they dangle in your face or what scraps from the table the master throws on the floor for you to eat, you will never be more than his African American! As close as Steven was, he never sat at the table with Calvin Candy.

Now, let's get to why Mr. Trump hates (*Assumption*) Barack and why black folks should love him for it. He doesn't like Barack because he's black, intelligent, empathic, classy, honest and a natural born leader. I will bet you dollars to doughnuts that if you dropped 20 people in a desert, jungle or in the middle of a forest fire who are rich, middle class or poor, black, white, Jew or gentile, Democrat or Republican (yep, I said Republican), and told them to choose a leader, we all know who they would choose. I'm pretty sure that the vote wouldn't even be close and as quiet as it may be if the vote was a secret ballot Donald Trump would vote for Barack Obama. This is what he absolutely hates. He abhors the fact that Barack Obama is everything that he is not.

He hates most black people because we acknowledge the game when we see it. It's not that we are too stupid to vote for him, it's that we are too smart to vote for him. We saw what he did to the Central Park 5 and continues to show his true colors through all the bankruptcies and stealing incidents. Black folks understand that.

Chapter One

BARACK HUMILIATED HIM AT THE CORRESPONDENTS' DINNER.

You remember the 2011 White House Correspondents dinner, all of the who's who in journalism was there. Now let's be honest, Barack had been waiting for this moment for a long time. Donald Trump had used every opportunity he could to run Obama's name in the mud. He questioned everything about Obama that he could. He accepted any lie, the conspiracy theory that somebody put out there, he almost said Obama was an alien. Yep for real, remember "whoever heard of him before this. Those grades in Harvard ain't real, I talked to his aunt, and she said he was born in Kenya, He threw everything he could and then some at Barack. Barack just let it go, until April 30, 2011. And now it was on and poppin. Obama got right in his business. Was it Vindictive, probably so. He earned that, and we call it "GET BACK!" Donald Trump earned it too. He hated that. Oh, did he hate that! He hates being laughed at, even in jest. He loves confrontation but he hates to be confronted. He loves Chaos, but he doesn't like dealing with conflict. The man is a walking conundrum. As quiet as it is kept, he is jealous of Obama. He sees all of Barack and wishes he could be him. I mean just think about. Obama hates confrontation and conflict but will confront any problem that he is confronted with. Barack hates Chaos but will not run from a fight. He will try to avoid it, but if he can't avoid it, he will confront it. So, Barack gave him what he had been wanting to give him for a while and Mr. Trump could not take it. But as bad as Barack served him, Seth Myers gave it to him much worse. But his hatred for Obama is unparalleled. It's not even close. You know what they say, it's a thin line between love and hate. No, let's take a look at what makes him hate Barack so much. I think the things that make him hate Obama are some of the same things that make him envy him so much.

Barack is smart, savvy, well-read, patriotic, caring, a great father, loved, and a man of integrity. I'm telling you; Trump wishes he could be the white version of Obama.

Sorry, that job has already been taken.

Now, why should it matter? Well, it should matter to black folks because the policies that he pushes will negatively affect most black folks. For instance, the so-called criminal justice reform bill has stepped up the attack on our community and locked up more people of color than Obama did in 8 years. It has given the police blanket immunity to stop and harass people of color all around the country with no fear of retribution. Let's just look at the climate, more people of color have been stopped, harassed and even killed by police and citizens for no other reason than melanin or the lack thereof. And my assumption is the election of Mr. Trump has empowered these people and reactions. Now that's is just my opinion or assumption, whichever is easier. It is a fact that Trump allowed the use of cages and detention camps for people of color at our borders and told brown people that our country was full but, at the same time, lobbied for European countries to send more immigrants. Well, that's just a start. We will examine more as we move on to the following chapters.

As my mamma used to say, "Let's keep it 💯 – No matter who it helps or hurts!"

BOTTOM LINE: If he didn't hate Barack Obama so much, black folks would have never known how good of a President Barack Obama was. And just as a side note, Mr. Trump needs to get out his feelings because he is doing too much (meaning "he is not doing enough of the right thing"). You ask how? No Pandemic Response Team – 90,000+ lives lost and a tanking economy. "Get out your feelings Orange Man!" Also, as quiet as it is kept, Kanye is in the same boat, Barack called him an A—Hole, and he has been acting like a skirt ever since.

Chapter Two

HE HATED JOHN MCCAIN.

HE HATED JOHN MCCAIN.

I said it twice so you could get the point. What? He hated John McCain? What does that have to do with Black folks? Just hold fast, I'm fittin' (LOL) to tell you, but first I'd like to know how a coward can question somebody's service. I like people that don't get caught!!! I mean, for real, they were all cowards. From his granddaddy who fled Germany because he was scared to fight (fact), all the way to his sons who took up the cowardice banner. I watched him say he read an article (read – what a joke) that informed him that the Kurds didn't help us doing World War II. I'd like to add that neither did his daddy, but we didn't throw his raggedy butt out – cold cowards – the whole clan of them. We have all seen the pictures of his momma smiling with that Klan robe (Fiction, it was photo shopped) on while standing with his daddy, but ask them to defend the country and each and every Trump will get ghost. I have heard people refer to him as the *Back to the Future Character*, Biff, but let's keep it real, Biff would fight. He just couldn't. Donald would run. I've seen the fear in his face when someone would run up on stage during his campaign rallies while he was campaigning. Let's not forget how he got checked by that black woman, the church Elder in Flint, Michigan when he tried to use their water crisis as a political stunt and then the next day, he tried to make like she was shivering. It was him, cold coward. John McCain may have been a lot of things, but a coward he was not. Now, why should we celebrate the person of John McCain?? First, let's give John McCain some credit. If John McCain is not John McCain, Barack Obama doesn't become President.

Remember October 10, 2008, an old lady began to talk about 44 in a very untrustworthy way (because of unwarranted anti-Muslimism hatred), and Senator McCain stepped in and corrected her? Now let that happen in today's climate, and Mr. Trump would have encouraged every white senior in America on why he shouldn't be President.

That's one reason, here goes at least six more:

- He was a patriot.

Flashback – July 28, 2018. Obamacare lies in the balance. Everybody waited on John McCain and what does he do, thumbs down.

- Now, why should we love this? If you have kids in college under the age of 26 and in school, guess what? Yep! They get to stay on your insurance! Can you imagine Jr. at school still thinking he has a chance at the NBA and breaks his ankle? Who pays? You, that's who! Thanks, John McCain, because Donald Trump and the Republicans don't care.

Let's look at pre-existing conditions:

- Diabetes (prevalent in the black community)
- Cancer (Breast cancer 20 to 50 percent that found a lump is included)
- Sleep Apnea
- COPD

And the list goes on and on – Thanks John McCain.

Isis would be on our doorsteps. While some people felt John McCain was a war hawk, and maybe so, it was McCain and that skirt Lindsey Graham who pushed the Obama Administration to use the Kurds as allies to fight Isis with little American footprints. How does that affect black people? Well, if you are ready to stay home and not go anywhere, it affects you. These people are determined to bring the fight to America.

Right here at your doorsteps.

Don't worry. I hate to say it, but they are coming. Donald Trump turned them loose. They will be here in a minute. If John McCain were living what happened in Syria would never have happened. He would have pimped slapped Lindsey Graham and told him he better get his boy. Coward is one name you could have never assigned John McCain.

KEEPING IT 100%: No John McCain, your kids don't have insurance, when momma finds that lump on her Breast, good luck with that. Terrorism well that's on the way. Real Black people issues. So, because he hated John being John served it right back to him. Win for us, America included.

Chapter Three

POSTER CHILD FOR ME TOO!

This is one of the main ones I can't understand. I'm going to need some help with this one. This man is on tape confessing to being a perpetrator of sexual assault/harassment. It's nothing in the world that kept me from not hearing that. He explicitly said, "When you are famous, they let you do it!"

He admitted it and then he comes out and says he doesn't remember saying it. WOW!! It's like he said, "Who are you going to believe? Me or your lying ass ears? "What does that have to do with black people? Well, for many years, black women have been marginalized when it comes to sexual exploitation. Yep, they have – white women are forced (there goes that pesky privilege again), black women want it. White women are subjected, black women are angry (for no reason).

You know it strikes me odd when I see people taking issue with Oprah for pulling Russell Simmons' card . The first thing people yelled was, "But they're supposed to be friends!" People should be more up in arms to think that he would be her friend and expect her to turn a blind eye We all know Mr. Trump and ole Russ were friends when Donald really started letting the world know his true colors. He wrote an open letter – please – what about the article/full page in the New York Times? Or trying to keep those innocent boys in a New York in jail? Or the discriminated suit brought against him by HUD? There are plenty of instances that illustrate his discriminatory ways. Birds of a feather do flock together. Mr. Trump is the admitted poster child and Russell is his first lieutenant. You don't get to do dirt and then pull the black card when you get exposed. There is enough privilege going around, so do you want to be known to house 'black rich privilege'? Go ahead, Oprah reveal them all! Russell Simmons, R. Kelly, Michael Jackson, Harvey Weinstein (move kind of slow on this one, though), Donald Trump, and whoever else you can find. Also find the time to go after all those that helped them commit the crimes – executive, managers, agents, family members, and whoever else was complicit in illicit behavior. Period!

AT THE END OF THE DAY: Black Folks don't like pedophilia!!! Period! The Alabama Senate Race showed that black women don't like it at all. They won't sweep it under the rug and for the most part they will call it out when they see it. Maybe it's because of what they know about slavery, rape and the degradation that women of color endured. For Heaven's sake don't end up in prison and let them find out, you are in big trouble.

Mr. Trump, from his own words, is the poster child of this behavior.

Just a little side note: Who fantasizes about dating their daughter?

NOW THAT'S FOUL

Chapter Four

HE WOKE UP ALL THE BLACK FOLKS TO THEIR (SO-CALLED) RACIST FRIENDS

Now you know, I mean you always thought maybe, but now you know. You know the ones who looked for reasons to justify George Zimmerman. The ones that find a reason to say that it had to be reasons for all these police shootings, or the ones that says all news outlets have fake news to justify watching Fox News, or the ones that says the confederate flags are about history or heritage – as if to say they didn't want black people to remain in bondage, or the ones that will tell you to your face that the only reason you voted for Barack is that he was black – like you don't have enough intelligence to vote for who you know is the best candidate or overlooking the fact that you have been voting for white people most of your life or that you can't remember back in 2008 and how this country was on the verge of financial collapse and it was Obama's policies that directly affected not only Black Folks life, but their life in such a positive way.

Now I will go out on the line and say not all these characteristics are racist but they are prejudice. The problem is when they are prejudice that leaves room for rationalization. It is like you forget about the ills that were associated with the 2008 recession, and you can accept the fact that he says the Obama Administration had a bunch of failed policies, when deep down you know that's not true. When he says that there was good and bad on both sides at the Neo Nazi rally in Charlottesville Virginia it makes you more tolerable with seeing confederate flags. When you start accepting his lies it makes it okay to be prejudice in your thinking so you can accept him and won't question his killing of the Iranian General because he made white Americans feel like people of color. He will do anything to push his mean spirited and racist agenda. Believe it or not, you have more black people starting to believe his way of thinking. Like, if things don't go their way it is because of little brown kids south of the border keeping them from living their American dream and what's even more astounding is that 1st generation Hispanic people are starting to feel this way also. Just a side note – You know what really knocks me off my feet How a Cuban (that's any immigrant for that matter) American can come here and "they think they are better than someone else." Oh really?

WOW – it is like Clarence Thomas taking advantage of all the affirmative action programs and then saying we don't need them. Unbelievable! From a common sense perspective point of view, you can't make this BS up. The one thing that is explicitly clear to me is the difference between racist and prejudice people in America is this, prejudice people will tolerate people of color. However, they will not invite you over for dinner, or they may, but they still think you should be grateful to be here and accept anything that is handed your way because we have done you a favor by letting you be here. They may or may not acknowledge the contributions of the slavery era, but if they do – they marginalize those contributors.

Now the racist is a whole different story; they don't want you here at all. They will accept other Europeans before you. The contributions of black America, it had nothing to do with me, so what that your whole history was created here. You and your kind were living in huts anyway.

It was a privilege to be raped and degraded by us. But now we want you out of here. Please leave as quickly as possible. I am always intrigued how people put black people in this cute little box. You can never label the slave descendants and other immigrants as the same concerning country identification. But when Martin Luther King, Jr. fought for freedom, he fought for everybody. One of his favorite quotes is also one of mine, "Injustice anywhere is a threat to justice everywhere." While this is true, our country or national origin is different, so when I hear racist say to a slave descendant to get out of my country, Donald Trump's lineage started here with his grandfather (in the early 1900), who was a coward who ran from Germany because he didn't want to fight in WW I – I guess that yellow streak runs in the family. My ancestor started here in the 1700's, and my origins were created here. My ancestors were raped, and from this, I was created. My mom was very light-skinned and would have been considered a house nigger, yet somebody from Russia coming here 18 months ago would be regarded as more American than I am.

1700 compared to 2019 0k! – I have heard transplanted Europeans at Trump Rallies yell, "Go back to where you come from." I mean really, get out of my country!

I am from Southern Maryland. One thing European Americans must understand is that just because their history of rape, sex trafficking – exploitation, thievery and murder make them uncomfortable, that is not my problem. And it shouldn't be. Because of that black people must understand we were created, it may be ugly, but it made us into who we are. So, you can't deny that part of history no matter how uncomfortable it is. Deny it not, nobody can! I cannot stress this enough. We must be prepared to tell the truth and record it.

NO DOUBT ABOUT IT: The cat is out the bag now. Black folks know who is who now. And they have Mr. Trump to thank for that. They would still be in the shadows. Thanks, Mr., Trump for making racism fashionable again. Now we know who you are.

Chapter Five

HE DOESN'T TELL THE TRUTH, AND HE HAS GOOD LAWYERS

Now think about all your friends, family members, associates, or even people you see on the news. You give them Donald Trump's lawyer. How many of them do you think would be walking the streets right now? For real, think about it if you would have defrauded someone out of $1,000.00. Do you think you would get a $10 fine and told not to do it again? Well, that's the gist of what took place at Mr. Trumps University and his charity in New York.

If you can steal $100,000 and have to pay a fine of 1% of your theft – that's a deal! I would take it every day of the week and twice on Sunday, especially when the judge says, "Don't do this anymore, until you find the next scheme." Now tell me that's not a great lawyer. Why should black people care about this? Well, it's kind of universal. If you are doing something you don't have any business doing, you should be investing at least 30% of your scheme into a lawyer. That's it and that's all. A good lawyer goes a long way in making sure crime does pay. Crime doesn't pay if you are black and have a court appointed attorney, but if you are black and have a great lawyer, your chances of crime paying off, goes up considerably. Now let's get to the 9,000 lies and counting. We always say all politicians lie. Not so fast. Making a promise and not being able to keep it is different from actually saying things like, I had the most external inaugural crowd in history," or "I rebuilt the military," – last one, "I didn't pay Stormy Daniels," or last one for real, "I didn't try to extort Ukraine," – all lies. Nonetheless, his supporters will tell you they all lie but you get the picture. His lying is on a whole other level. He is the father of all lies. He knows it, his followers know it, and we all know it.

THE FACT OF THE MATTER: Black folks have been saying for years that the Justice System is rigged against people of color. No matter how much data they collect there are still a lot of people around (in the black community) who say as long as you do what you are supposed to do it will all work out. Some feel that all criminals will get their just do. Well Mr. Trump has shown black folks that what they have been saying all along is true; however, he has also let them know that a very good lawyer goes a long way when it comes to maintaining your freedom. Let's keep this straight, I am not condoning criminal activity, but I am saying if you do need a lawyer make sure you get the best.

Chapter Six

HE SHOWED US HOW MUCH OUR VOTE REALLY COUNTS

Big D, I take my hat off for you on this one my friend. We didn't have an understanding, but you did what so few have been unable to do for years. In your win in 2016, we lost it for the country we say we love so much. I mean, that's at least 2 million voters that did not vote in the last election. If we break that up into eight states what would the Senate and the presidency look like?

Give Pennsylvania, Michigan, Wisconsin, Ohio, Florida, North Carolina, and Georgia, that's not even counting the senators in Colorado and Arizona. What does that mean for black American? What does that mean for real prison reform? I mean real prison reform! Does it fix the holes in Obama care (public option), universal background check for guns (less mass shootings), prescription drug price reform, student loan reform, banking reform (4 billion in overdraft profit for banks), better climate control legislation, less dependency on foreign oil (keep us out of Saudi Arabia and acting as their body guards and Iran wouldn't be getting ready to have nuclear weapons) .That's just a small taste of how things would have been if we voted in 2016 like we voted in 2012. Would you like proof? Facts – Black women in the state of Alabama kept the state from putting an alleged generational pedophile in the US Senate, mind you that the state is between 35 to 40% Black. Mr. Trump campaigned for him, and the sister's said like Rosa Parks – "Nah! We can say black lives matter (and they do), but black votes matter just as much!"

TO BE HONEST WITH YOU: We all have paradigm moments in our life that moves us in different directions and places us on the path for where we need to go. Mine was at the MLK center in Atlanta when I saw the exhibits of the people who put their life on the line for me to have the right to vote and determine what direction the country should go in. This was one of the most enlightening, powerful and defining moments of my life.

Mr. Trump urged black people to vote for him by asking, "What the hell do you have to lose?" Those are his words, not mine. Now we know and everybody else does too! I can list hundreds of things we have lost or were on the path to lose if it were not for Nancy Pelosi. The one thing that Mr. Trump and the Republican

Party have done on a consistent basis is try to take away something our parents, grandparents and ancestors fought and died for, OUR VOTE!!! They attempted to come up with different schemes and strong-arm tactics laced with intimidation, yet black people have no clue on how much their vote really counts. Just to reiterate to everyone, "YOU'RE VOTE COUNTS!" Everybody Black and White!!!

Chapter Seven

HE MADE BLACK AMERICA ENGAGE IN THE POLITICAL PROCESS MORE

Over the last three years I have encountered a lot of young black people talking about politics. The discussion was not limited to things pertaining to the president but the entire political process. I can't ever remember that happening before. I even saw a very insightful rap video about the whole political process and the different branches of government; it was very good. If Donald Trump has done nothing else, he has united us under one flag or thought: The vast majority of black folks *don't like Donald Trump!* So, since black folks don't like him, they have all combined to do one thing- and that is to defeat him. Now there are a variety of reasons why black folks don't like him. Some valid and some not so much. Some black folks don't like him because of the Central Park Five situation (taking out an ad in the New York Times to try and keep five innocent boys of color in jail even though they were innocent) Facts. Some black folks don't like him because he insults black folks for no other reason than he can. (black people are too stupid and dumb to vote for me)

Assumption. Some don't like him because he puts a lot of effort into bringing down positive black men every chance he gets (Barack Obama, LeBron James, Don Lemon, Steph Curry) Facts. He has no reason to invest this negative energy towards these positive men other than the fact that they don't support him or that they are black (Assumption). He attempts to question their intelligence. And this is from a man who reads from about a 9th grade level at best (fact – I see him struggle, I don't need a pundit to tell me otherwise), but when I look at this man, I see a very insecure person who is uncertain about is his appearance, his education, and his poor business practices. So, he will say, "I'm doing a great job," over and over again, when in fact that is not the case. My simple question for supporters of Trump is what has he done to make this economy great? I'll wait!! Or make your life better personally.

The fact is the economy was humming along well before he took office, (Facts) period! And what does he do? He gives the top 10% in this country a generous tax cut. What do they do? They invest it in their workforce? Nope. They invest it in their infrastructure for better work force productivity. Nope. They use the profits from the tax cuts to buy back the stock in their company to get more profits and make more money. It's greed at its finest

(70% of all profits from the 2017 tax cut for the top 10% went to company buybacks – Facts). What's more surprising is that Trump is taking credit for something he didn't do. It really shouldn't really surprise me, but it does. That's been happening in America since black people got here. Black America have contributed a great deal to this country. By a wide margin, they have contributed Economically, Emotionally, Spiritually and Socially. But when you check the American and World history books, the information provided is limited to a paragraph or two. It's as if the history, to include the sacrifices and contributions made by the people of color in the United States are overlooked and underappreciated. I mean you got to be kidding me. So, when I see Mr. Trump minimize the achievements of the first black president of the United States, it doesn't surprise me. It's the same ole song we've been hearing and seeing for years. What surprises me is that the black folks with a voice hardly ever come to Barack's defense, and the terrible part about it is, it's not a hard argument to win. In 2008 when this country was on the verge of financial calamity, there were over 40 million black people in this country. You saw the same thing I saw; you saw how he turned it around, but still, black folks struggled with explaining what they saw and what happened. I mean they really struggle. You even have Kanye "Slavery was a Choice "West still never has anything good to say about Obama. He wants him to apologize for calling him a asshole for being a asshole. So now he says Obama could have done more to curtail the violence in Chicago. Excuse me, but let me keep it a buck with you, Chi-Town has a lot of heavy hitter from their when it comes to people of color (Chance the Rapper , Common , R Kelly , Kanye , D. Wade , Derrick Rose, The Nation Of Islam and the list goes on) , but black folks put the messiah label on Barack more than anybody . It's almost like, he could save a hundred kids from drowning and some black folks would be on the side of the river saying, "but look their clothes are all wet and they will probably catch a cold!" Can somebody else do some of the heavy lifting.

Some black folks help Trump and his supporters out by helping to build false narratives and co-signing on some of these outrageous claims. One of the most open and honest and questions you can ask any Trump supporter, black or white and it will stop the average one in his or her tracks is, "What policy or action has he (Mr. Trump) implemented that has helped you or been beneficial to the country as a whole?" And, you know what? Most can't answer that question. I always wait to be asked the same question, but few would dare to ask because it would be way to easy, I mean way to easy. Let's look at a couple of small facts. In 2010 the average tax refund was $3,003. The average refund in 2018 was $2,781. Those are the numbers, period! It should be more, but it's less. Now when black people see that or they start counting, well they can count so when Mr. Trump say black folks are too stupid to vote for him, well if it's going to cost me $300 to vote for him, I will take the dumb label and keep my $300.

WHEN ALL SAID AND DONE: Most black folks have been satisfied with letting things go, but not this one. Baby Boomers, Generation X, and Millennials have all had a firsthand look for themselves so they know what happened in 2008 and 2009. They lived it and they remember, so when he trashes Barack Obama, they figure it's because of one reason and one reason only. At the end of the day numbers don't lie, and when Mr. Trump and his co-defendants come out and continuously lie, it causes them to develop an emotional dislike for him. At this point the fire has spilled over into the political discourse, and have made people question and explore, and from that exploration comes engagement. So, when an educated voter appears, all should worry; Republicans and Democrats alike. Republicans should worry because of policy; Democrats should worry because of their laziness and cowardice. The status quo will not last long in this environment. If you think it's a joke ask Roy Moore in Alabama. It's been a hiccup here and there, but for the most part the anti-establishment train is moving. If I am Republican and believe in mean spirited policies, making sure rich donors are my first priority, that healthcare is a privilege and not a right, I also believe that I have the right to buy a assault rifle, go into a school and kill 20 plus little kids or rent a room in Las Vegas and use a assault rifle and kill and wound over 200 plus people. That's all good. They will say that's not how it is but those are the facts , and facts do matter , But if I am a democrats and I am too lazy to have a town hall meeting to explain to people where their tax dollars are going and why some of these republican policies are bad for me and the country. I would really start to worry – Republican or Democrat!!! Thanks, Mr. Trump because if you had not given all that money to the top 5 or 10%, we probably would have never known what a stock buyback was all about.

Chapter Eight

HE SHOWED WHO THE REAL UNCLE TOM'S AND STEPHAN'S REALLY WERE.

Something that blows me away more than anything is when rich people of color are willingly to turn a blind eye to his racist ways. I've always wanted to ask Ray Lewis, Steve Harvey, Jim Brown, and Kanye West if they think they are excluded from his comments alleging that black folks are too stupid to vote for him. I wonder if they think he's not talking about them, or if they think because they have a few more dollars than others, that they are exempt from the name calling or degradation, or marginalization of people of color.

Especially when he comments on the low IQ's of African Americans – naw, he not talking about you. Nope, we all know you are a scholar.

Don't worry! When they began to try and purge the country of all people of color, Stephen Miller is going to let you stay. He has a waiver for you and that 30% of the Hispanic population that voted for him! Let's not forget that 5% of fine people of India/Pakistani descent – he's going to let you stay, too. Plus, you just brought 3 billion dollars in arms from the USA (none of it goes into the US Treasury, it goes to the defense contractor and his campaign contributors). So, as he tears down every person of color he can find regularly, don't worry, he's not talking about you.

Remember Steven from *Django*. He was exempt. He hated black people more than Calvin Candy did. Calvin Candy looked at things from a money point of view. Steven looked at things more from a color and class situation. It always strikes me odd how some of these guys can be such ferocious warriors in their chosen fields, but when it comes time to stand tall, they seem to shrink. I couldn't believe when Ray Lewis suggested that Kaepernick should apologize – apologize for what? For trying to save my son's life and his son's life? He didn't commit a crime. He didn't provide a getaway vehicle for two homicide suspects. What's one other thing we can thank Mr. Trump for? We can thank him for showing how great of a divide there is within the black community.

It has always been about class until life throws you a curveball and reminds you what color you are. It is at that point that you are forced to run back and look for cover. It takes very little courage to follow the crowd.

Steven forgot who he was until all the white folks were gunned down and he realized it was time to try and sneak out the door. Most Uncle Toms' only want to be black when it's convenient. They already know where they want to fit in at. You know the ones who really don't like being black and think they are better than the _regular_ black folks. It is a class thing. I have quite a few Hispanic friends, and you would be surprised at how many of them think they are better than other Hispanic people from Guatemala, El Salvador, Honduras, and Nicaragua. I mean, it is surprising. The closer they look to being white, the more they believe they are superior to others.

Melanin determines a lot of who they think they are, and the lack of it makes them feel like they are better than their own kind, so the more they put their own down, the more they think they will be accepted. Never mind, they are both looking for opportunity. Still, they think they are better. They were able to take advantage of the Reagan amnesty program, my skin is a little paler, so I am better than you and, in most cases, black folks too because they are ungrateful. So thus, they wear their Hispanic Uncle Tom's badge proudly. Donald Trump is my man. I can't wait to get my waiver. Stephen Miller got me. Same with Middle Eastern, Indians, Asians, and even some Africans.

They think they are better. That's it, and that's all.

JUST TO KEEP IT REAL WITH YOU: One thing for certain and two things for sure, a lot of what has happened to black folks have been perpetuated by black folks, some knowing and some unknowing. But all the same it happened and still happens. Why is that? First, we have to figure out what motivates the Uncle Tom. I think for the most part it's about the BAG (Money). They either want it, or afraid they are going to lose it. Others may say that's its mind conditioning (Steven from *Django*), just wanting to believe that a certain group or race of people will have your best interest at heart, no matter what they have shown you in the past. But I think it's more so the bag and the greed for the bag. Now black folks know for sure who some of these people are, no matter the motivation. It is ok that a lot of these people are in the entertainment industry. Continue to be entertained, just be careful about when these people give advice, check their motive. I would say they probably should not have earned your trust if they are telling you to do anything but vote! I Don't trust them. They earned the side-eye!!!

Chapter Nine

HE SHOWED US WHAT FAKE CHRISTIANS AND THE ANTI-CHRIST REALLY LOOKED LIKE

Now, this is the one. It is common knowledge that black people are the most religious people in the world, period! For instance, in Africa, let's start with the country of Nigeria, you can find some of the richest pastors in the world. Twelve of the wealthiest pastors in the world are people of color, add Benny Hinn, and you have 13! That's factual. What does that have to do with anything? Well, let's start with black people having faith in their religious leaders.

How many times have you heard a black person use their pastor or a well-known religious leader to establish a fact? It happens every day and twice on Sunday.

Now I said religious leader, and I didn't say men or women of God. I mean real people of God - religious leaders and men or women of God, there is a difference.

Paul (Saul) the Pharisee (religious leaders), and Paul the apostle where two different people. Same principle, but when we look at the religious leaders and how they placate to becomes complicit in Mr. Trumps Shenanigans. It gives black people pause. You have a few tokens, but for the most part, black pastors have stayed silent or spoken out against him. Still, the white religious leaders in this country support him as a whole, and the lengths they will go to so they can excuse his blasphemy is unbelievable at best. Their excuse are laughable, saying that all politicians lie is the most troublesome one. Lying about something that people can see (like facts and the truth) and making a promise that you can't keep is different. It is still a lie, but it is different. This is what you call a false equivalence, you know the saying apples and oranges is the same because they are both fruit and they both have Vitamin C. To justify his whoremonger (a person who has dealings with prostitutes, especially a sexually promiscuous man -Fact) ways and this kind of behavior is spiritual homicide at best. Mind you, these are supposed to be the type of people we look to for spiritual guidance, "PLEASE "there will be a reckoning, but remember they are religious leaders, not spiritual leaders. Now let's take a look at some of the other things they are at the very least ignoring. His most glaring weakness from a spiritual perspective is his lack of love for anything or anybody that doesn't affect him. He seems to have no empathy at all. None, Nada -Zero!!! I mean, Jesus Christ's number one commandment was to love unconditionally, simple – that is usually meant for believers to be empathetic (that wasn't a suggestion or request, but a commandment). I'd love for someone to show me a time when this guy displays any type of empathy. A tree is really known by the fruit that it bears. If anybody needs that fruit to survive, you will starve. Still not a peep from the religious leaders. Now I want everybody that believes he has never pressured or paid for an abortion, please raise your hand. I mean, this guy has said creepy things about his own daughter. He mentioned that he would date his own daughter. You don't think that's at least creepy. So, if you think black people don't see this, you are crazy or as one of my close friends would always say when somebody wanted to do or say something stupid or dumb "you must be outside your mind!"

Remember, black women, are the sole reason we don't have an alleged pedophile in the US Senate from the great state of Alabama – roll tide! So, while most black people have some sort of understanding of basic biblical principles and believe in a higher power, they still rely on the convictions of their Pastor and much to the detriment of Mr. Trump, they have been noticeably quiet. Regardless of if he wants to believe it or not, it has a lot to do with how he treated Barack Obama and other people of color (Hispanics included) You can even add in how he went to Saudi Arabia and put his hands on that globe, you would never see Obama do that. Well, black folks are watching, and they are going to vote.

I WOULD BET YOU DOLLARS TO DOUGHTNUTS: I was talking to a friend the other day. She said she doesn't care too much for Paula White anymore. Some will admit it and some won't admit that Mr. Trump killed their brand, especially in the black community. I think that's great, not because she is a Trump supporter but because if you are spiritual/religious leader and if your brand does anything but glorify God, it should be destroyed. If it condones, glorifies, exalts or praises any man- it's not of God. It's for lack of another word idol worshipping and blasphemy. So, I will bet anybody who wants to if Donald Trump can recite 10 scriptures, I will pay you. As a matter of fact, since the Bible is his favorite book, let's make it 5 scriptures. I'll wait! But thanks again Mr. Trump for exposing these hypocrites for who they are – Appreciate it Chump, sorry I mean Champ.

Chapter Ten

WHITE PRIVILEGE

Well, last but not least, white privilege, where do I start and where do I end? This man is the epitome of white privilege. Let's look at the facts. He went to the University of Penn now the Wharton School of Business. Now you tell me if you think he went to Penn and graduated. Please raise your hand. I can't believe people think he went to this school and graduated. I mean, I watch this man regularly on TV and can see that he can barely read, and when I say barely, I am being very generous. Really, he can't.

I mean, we all see it, and I don't need anyone to come and tell me any differently. I don't need a political pundit, prognosticator or a 3rd grade English teacher. Needless to say, if you think black people can't see it as well then you must be on narcotics. He can't read, period or as my niece says **PERIODT**!!! (Hyperbole, he can read a little bit. Very little.) You hear his fans talk about he does not like the teleprompters because he likes to talk and be honest. He does not like the teleprompters because he can't read, and he struggles to learn from it.

People can see it, but because he's white he gets a pass, plain and simple. Don't think so? Name me one black person who struggles like that and could rise to national prominence. I'll wait. I look at other candidates who also struggled to read, but it is not as bad as Mr. Trump. Noticeably, Mr. Bush struggled, and there were others. We all know it would never work in the black community, that's plain and simple. I watched as commentator after commentator said Mr. Obama was excellent in reading the teleprompter, almost trying to diminish him.

He can read, shouldn't we all be able to read, would that make me elite because I can read? WOW – what if I can read and write? That must make me super elite! Pure white privilege!! Now think about this, how can a man who ducks the war not be considered a coward? Please enlighten me. He deferred four times for school and got two extras after that. Name me one black man who would have been able to do that, get away with it, and rise to be one of the most powerful men in the world. I'll wait. Again, let's remember Muhammad Ali declined to go into the military because of political and religious reasons, and this country tried to break him, and took away some of his prime boxing years. Regardless of this, Ali held on to his beliefs and stood on his principles. And paid a very heavy price for it. It took him years to recover from this episode in his life. When Ali died, he was beloved around the world, but when he was younger, not so much (Facts).

Still, Mr. Trump got elevated, one gets ostracized the other elevated, unbelievable! Now I can go on and on about how he insults people on a regular basis while his co-defendants state how he is a counter puncher. We all know he starts most controversies. I have always wondered how a man can insult people simply because he can and does not expect people to be offended. I need help with that one. I can talk about how most think his relationship with Russia would be considered treason at best and espionage at worst.

Name me one black person who would be able to get away with any of this.

This country was ready to go to war with Cuba for buying arms from Russia. Mr. Trump lets them parade through the White House as if they own it, and some in Congress think he should get the Noble Peace Prize for it. I mean, for real. Now, do you think black folks don't see this? The treasonous behavior, insults, the white privilege, hiding his taxes, demonizing other people of color (Hispanic and Latino) encouraging police to violate black people's civil rights (people died for those laws) and condoning and encouraging voter suppression laws.

Oh yeah, one last question, for every father, in America white, black, Jew or Gentile, do you not find it real foul and creepy for a man to fantasize about dating his daughter? I find this more than a little disturbing, but sickening. I can't think of anybody I know who would feel otherwise. I got loads of white privilege scenarios, but it would take another 50 pages, and I think most get the picture!!

YOU BEST BELIEVE: You best believe black folks know what white privilege looks like, they know what it sounds like, and they know what it smells like. They don't need anyone to tell them what it is. You would be hard pressed to find any black person in this country who has not been touched in some kind of way by this atrocity. Mr. Trump not only displays it, but flaunts it and when Black folks see it; they hate it because it reminds them of the history that wasn't so kind to them and their ancestors. So, you have to appreciate the fact that he feels comfortable enough to flaunt it. His supporters may love it but black folks never will, even his so called trans-actionable (so-called) friends may go along with it for obvious reasons (the bag) but they don't like it either.

Epilogue

Now let's be very clear about something. In the beginning of this book I gave you a definition to make it easier to understand the BS we see on a day to day basis. I would like everybody to remember one thing that's very important. One of the biggest News Outlets right now is Facebook and Instagram. That's a Fact, but what's cloudy is where they get their information from. Most of the time its unverified, so be very careful on what's coming from these social media outlets and what you choose to believe Twitter fits this category also. Just so you will get an understanding on what I am talking about, doing the Covid-19 pandemic I saw a article on Facebook stating that Russia was letting Lions roam the streets to enforce their quarantine order. Do you know I had at least 2 friends that actually believed this! Facebook will let this go and if you go for it, that's on you. Don't forget about the Trump supporter who raided Ping Pong Comet to break up the child sex ring that Hilary Clinton was running. Some of these Lies, yep I called them lies! Not Conspiracy theories, they are Lies, Plain and Simple!!!! Don't Forget about the horrible lie Alex Jones told when he said it was Fake News and that those

Little kids where not killed in Connecticut. How can anybody still be his friend. He is lower than any earth worm that I know of. Pure Sickness. And for some of the so-called Faith leaders who says Donald Trump is sent from God – and I quote "These six things do the Lord HATE, yea seven are an abomination unto him; A PROUD LOOK (narcissist), a Lying Tongue!" Proverbs 6;16 - 19) Now that's Bible! So just asking for a friend, the things that God despise in people he sent as a blessing to America. Now if you believe that I have some prime real estate in the Florida swamp to sale you. Opps my bad you not Russian and I am not Donald Trump (Fact).

So just a small recap:

Facts – Something that exists – Real – an actual occurrence

Truth- The body of real things, events and fads. Actuality

Reality- The world or state of things as they actually exist

Actuality – Existing Conditions or facts

Now for the Grimsey:

Hyperbole – Exaggeration, embellishment, overstatement

Innuendo – An oblique allusion

Disingenuous – Lacking in honesty, giving a false appearance of simple frankness

Platitudes – A remark in a speech or writing that is overused and has no originality (cliché)

Lies – Distortions, leaving out relevant info, a false statement made with deliberate intent to deceive

Speculation – The forming of a theory or conjecture without firm evidence

Fake – Not Genuine, counterfeit

Bullshitter - (Vulgar) – Someone who lies or exaggerates a lot, especially in order to get noticed.

Fake News – A form of news consisting of deliberate misinformation or hoaxes spread via traditional news media (print or broadcast) or social media.

Let's be real clear about a few things, Just because a specific person said something, that does not make that statement right or truthful even if it is expressed with passion, purpose, or whispered. It does not matter. I had a friend who told me the truth needs no support, and it doesn't. Lies, falsehood, innuendoes, and being disingenuous all need a crutch to stand on, or someone else to embellish their statements. Truth or facts stand on its own and can be tested through time. And it has. Slavery was a horrific time in American History. That's a fact! No matter how uncomfortable America may be with the truth, this era will always be a stain on America. The Holocaust was perpetrated by a whole country, led by an evil mad man simply because he blamed the failure of a country on a group of people who were vulnerable. Germany lost World War I because of Germany (listen up white Supremist). They went in to depression because of Germany. I hope you see where I'm going with this. Donald trump was a failed business man because of Donald Trump. He failed in business because of Donald Trump! The Taj Mahal and Las Vegas casinos failed because of Donald Trump. Trump University failed because of Donald Trump! Trumps Steaks and Wine Failed because of Donald Trump. Trump Airlines failed Because of Donald Trump! Trump Charites failed because of Donald Trump! These are all facts. He was in charge, they were his companies, they all failed, and that's just the tip of the iceberg. It is public record and facts and truth needs no support. No Mexican or Hispanic immigrant, African-American, Hispanic Judge, News Media or any other race, or group of people has contributed to his failings. He did it all by himself.

Now he has had two failed marriages and has raised some terrible, greedy, self-absorbed, non-empathic, dumb kids. Now that's just speculation, me and nobody else have facts to back that up (Now we maybe speculate about the kids because of the tree is known by the fruit that it bears). Some even say he committed sexual assault. At this point, that's just speculation even though over 16 women have come out and say he made unwanted sexual advances toward them. All of those are allegations. If he did commit these acts, where are the charges or criminal complaints? You do know you can file a criminal complaint against anyone even if the statues of limitations have expired; file the complaint.

Is he a human pig, absolutely! He admitted on tape that he will stick his hand in the panties of women without asking simply because he is famous. That's not only piggish type of behavior, but it is disturbing. Men in power have been getting away with this type of behavior for years, but that's not an excuse for their behavior. The fact is that they do it and get away with it, but the, "Me Too Movement" is hot on their case.

Now, let's talk about how politicians use words to manipulate and distort actuality and how society accepts it. Black people will go by what they see. Do you think they don't know most white politicians only come into their community during election season? Black people, for the most part, just pick the lesser of the two evils. And I say that loosely, that can be one of the most disingenuous statements made in the political arena today because they all are not the lesser of the two evils. Some are really decent people. Just like all preachers are not pimps, some are really Men of God. And some just develop a thirst for power and have no idea how to control the urge for more. But black folks recognize this. So, every now and then they become inspired by one who appears to be genuine, and will rally behind the said candidate, but most of the time they will come to the party late, if they come at all.

Make no mistake about it; they know what's going on. They just have no clue on how powerful and important their vote is. I'll say this one more time for the people in the back who may be sleeping: If it wasn't for black women, the state of Alabama was going to send an alleged pedophile to the US Senate.

Think 2008, Barack Obama. Most black people will tell you they didn't support Obama in the beginning. It was the white electoral that opened their eyes and gave him a look and see. Once they saw that, they were all in. Now think Hilary Clinton. Most black people liked her, but to stand in line to vote for her, nope, wasn't that inspired to do that. She was probably, as Obama said, the most prepared candidate to have ever run for the presidency in modern times. She checked most of the boxes, and I said most. But, unfortunately for America, a lot, not all, but most, only move when they are inspired, especially black folks. Watch the way black folk support their churches on Sunday mornings, and use their pastor as a prayer book, and factual resource. They have to be inspired, it's unfortunate but it's true.

That's just how they roll. One last thing before I move on to the fact and fiction part of this book. There is a difference between a politician that promises to get better gun laws and work like the dickens to get it passed, but fails and one who says he's going to work on getting better gun laws with the NRA and never even attempt to do anything.

They both lied, but one tried, and the other just flat out lied. Black folk see the difference in intent, but most people will try to say that all politicians lie. While this is true, one intends on doing the right thing while the other just wants power and to please campaign donors. I will say this, unfortunately, the power-hungry donor pleasers have been the most effective. I will say it's kind of disheartening when you see a smart hard working politician that you know that's there for the people (Alexandria Ocasio Cortez to name one) and works tirelessly for her constituents and then you watch political pundits try to character assassinate them just to further the agenda of a candidate who is only interested in power and not people . they will use personal failings or perceived failings to distract you, Black and White folks. Later on, in this book I will go over some of these candidates and we all should ask ourselves why do we still vote for some of these people. A lot of people will not like it but some of the poorest towns, counties and cities have US Senators they have become Multi-Millionaires and have kept you without livable wages, healthcare and a decent standard of living , and the crazy thing is they do it on our dime. OUR DIME!!! We pay them to get rich. The vast majority of these Senators are White Old Men and Most are Republican. Some are Democrats, but it doesn't make a difference, incompetence, corruption and greed knows no color or political affiliation. Just a small side note, I was mildly heartbroken when I saw the democratic candidate for Governor from the state of Florida get caught up in an alleged scandal and check himself in a substance abuse rehabilitation center, he seemed to be a rising political star in the democratic political party. But simply put if what they say about him is true this type of behavior is unacceptable no matter what color you are or whatever political party you represent. One thing I will not allow myself to do is make allowances for people simply because I may like them and because I think they may have a good political platform. He made a mistake and he apologized for it. Black folks let's keep it 100%! Remember Jesus didn't give the women that was about to be stoned to death for committing adultery a pass. After he saved her life, he told her to go and sin no more.

Let me be clear on a few things, like I said before the truth needs no support. I am not lying on the man and when I saw him on TV, I really thought I was looking at a future presidential candidate. And I still like him and I am praying for him. Just so you will know my mom was a alcoholic and in the neighborhood she frequented she was known as a drunk. But you know what I stilled loved her. She was undoubtedly one of the smartest people I knew. I mean real smart; she could read a 500-hundred-page novel in a day or two and could tell you everything about it 2 or three years after she had read it. She made sure I could read and articulate my thoughts in a meaningful and thoughtful way at an early age. I loved her and I do honor her but she was an alcoholic. So, I don't give Andrew Gillum a pass for three reasons, first is he is a grown man- as we use to say in our neighborhood Bone-Up Cuz! Get up and brush yourself off and get back at it! God, your family and this country needs you. Second – "To whom much is given, much is required!" But check this there is something called redemption everybody in this world has done something they are ashamed up and had to ask forgiveness for. Except Donald Trump.

And last but not least if I give him a pass, I have to give Rush Limbaugh a pass. He not only was a Dope Fiend but he turned his house keeper into a co-conspirator (don't forget a Hispanic house keeper). And just think this racist Dope Fiend once said anybody using drugs should be incarcerated (as the little girl in the movie Bless the Child said, "After You"). That's a fact, he said it drug users should go to jail and he was convicted for buying and possessing opiates. But still he received the highest civilian honor given to an American citizen in this country. Now somebody tell me that white privilege doesn't exist. Child Please! It exists more so now than almost ever. Now you have other ethnic groups coming to America and thinking they are more deserving than the average black people that was born and raised here and who's ancestor helped build America into what it is today. But that's another story I will tackle in the next book – "We Are Not The Same!" "The miseducation of the minority immigrant in America!"

The reason why Mr. Trump's game doesn't resonate in the black community is a twofold thing – one is Game recognize Game and two is that black folks remember the 2008 election. And most black folk will reflect on that historic night and it seems that Mr.

Trump use every opportunity he can to void that historic night and they don't appreciate someone trying to void it. Never mind the fact that Barack has proven to be the best President this country has had, in at least my lifetime, if not ever. So, they see how he has been treated, and it has resonated. Mr. Trump tried to damage Obama, but he forgot that black folk was here, they lived through it, they experienced it, and so he can say what he wants. Facts are facts, and when you live it, it makes a difference, no matter what you say.

The truth needs no support. Michelle Obama was a lawyer that graduated from one of the most prestigious universities in this country. Melania was a soft-porn actress. Barack Obama was President of the Harvard Law Review, Trump had to threaten the university he went to with a lawsuit if they released his transcript to the public. These are the facts, and I am not trying to put her down, but those are the facts. Black folks can see and hear. Michelle has grace and intellect. Melania, not so much. Anytime you have to plagiarize someone else's speech, that's not graceful or eloquent. Black folks see this. Mr. Obama was a lawyer who became President and can read. While that doesn't mean you are superior, that does suggest that you are educated. On the other hand, Mr. Trump had to threaten University's not to release his transcripts.

Those are facts. This is not fake news. This is just the truth, no matter how much someone may not like it. Just because someone may be displeased with hearing those facts, it won't change its actuality, and black folk know it. They need to thank Mr. Trump for not hiding it, but for being candid about who he is and most of his supporters are. I heard a TV host say the red mega hat was the new KKK white hood. It may or may not be, but rest assured, the symbol of hatred from that time sure resonated with black people. Most black people have never seen a Klan in real life but have experienced racism, and they know racist rhetoric when they hear it, and it comes from Mr. Trump and his supporters regularly.

Now, let's talk facts and fiction.

Facts – October 2009, Unemployment 10.2 – 9 months after Obama was inaugurated President; the country began its recession in 2007. From 2007 to November 2009, it lost approximately 2.5 million jobs – **Facts.**

Fact – GDP

2008 – 0.1%
2009 – 2.5%
2010 – 2.6%
2011 – 1.6%
2012 – 2.2%
2013 – 1.8%
2014 – 2.5%
2015 – 2.9%
2016 – 1.6%
2017 – 2.4%
2018 – 2.9%
2019 – 2.3%

Now, if you take out the first two years for the recession the Obama's economy grew at 2.17%, which is kind of good considering what he inherited, the first two years he had to stop the bleeding – these are facts.

Now, to Mr. Trump's credit, the economy grew at an average of 2.6%, not bad, kind of good to be truthful. But he inherited an economy that was humming, and I do mean thriving, to say the least, compared to what Obama inherited. Yet, he comes out and tells people time and time again he inherited a mess – Please… He has to be living in an alternate universe. We say facts – unemployment 10.2% at its worst, GDP a minus 2.5%. GM and

Chrysler filing bankruptcy, over 50 banks going under, countless other business was going under.

Black folks were here, but just in case some forgot – Thanks Mr. Trump for the stroll down memory lane. I'm sure black America appreciates your efforts, but one question that always stumps Trump supporters, and it gets them every time is, "What policy, legislation, or law did he pass or champion that made this economy so great under his leadership?" I will wait, the only thing that he can speak of is this great tax cut, you know the one where Americans receive $500 less in their refund and get $18.00 more on their by-weekly paychecks. That's his crowning achievement. Data shows it, like Nino Brown (New Jack City) says, "The rich get richer and the poor get nothing," even though his language was a little more colorful. But the rich, after promising to invest in their company (employees and infrastructure), but 70% of them took the money and bought back stock in their company, that's a fact. Pure Greed.

Now when you ask about what Obama did to make things move along, let's talk facts:

- First Time Homebuyers Program, $10,000 Tax Credit

- Cash for Clunkers, $5,000 Tax Credit

- Cash for appliances, $1,500 Max. benefit

    - Homebuyer Reinvestment Program – to help people stay in their homes and stop foreclosures

- The Automotive Industry Financing Program – which was paid back (over 1 million jobs were lost because of this crisis)

- Enacted a Better Troubled Asset Relief Program (TARP) – to ensure better accountability to get the taxpayer money back – everybody paid the money back except Wells Fargo (why am I not surprised)

- Affordable Care Act (Obama Care)

    - Every parent in America needs to thank Obama, kids get to stay on insurance until the age of 26 (just think of all the collage kids that would be in trouble)

    - Save people with Pre-existing conditions

- Rebates if you stay healthy
- Global Pandemic Response Team (more about that later)

And for real, that's just some. I'm not even going to talk about the Lilly Leadbetter Act (executive order for woman to make the same as men that do the same job, this shouldn't even be an issue) and some of the other domestic policies and foreign policies he championed, just to put it mildly.

He restored American exceptionalism, and Mr. Bin Laden is no longer roaming the world. All of these are facts, plain and simple. As I have said before, the truth and fact cannot be argued or disputed. It is what it is, whether I like it or not. The same goes for you, like my Uncle used to say, "Man up." My cousin (his son) would always say, "Bone up!" (Deal with it) The bottom line is that the truth needs no support! I can never understand why people never run on the Obama record, they act like he presided over a recession or created one. If Donald Trump would have turned this country around like that, this country would have started carving his picture on Mount Rushmore and the Republicans would have commissioned it.

I finally heard Nancy Pelosi, after one State of the Union put out some facts. But what are you afraid of? Black folks just don't like him because he was black (it helps), he was successful and he saved the country from financial ruins, and he did it with class and with a beautiful and successful woman by his side. – Fact!! One of the reasons they don't like Mr. Trump is because he tries to destroy that with his lies and distortions. I have named countless other reasons also but I would be lying if I said this didn't rank high on the list. One thing he and nobody can never take away from black folks is the pride they feel when they see Barack Hussein Obama!

Voter Guide

Let's run through a quick handicapping of the upcoming 2020 election.

I have heard this is the most critical election in our lifetime, even more important than 2008 (recession/depression). I'm afraid so, as far as it goes for black people. Ask yourself, do you want to continue going back to when racism and bigotry were not only condoned but encouraged. I'm afraid that is where we are headed. Some have already surmised you will never be able to put that toothpaste back in the tube. Maybe or maybe not – I do know that if we keep on at this pace with the current administration, it will get much worse. Much, much worse. I don't mean to scare you, but I do intend to wake you up to the urgency of NOW – black folk will have to vote – plain and as straightforward as I can be. Vote as if Obama were running again. This victory will have to be decisive and resounding. Otherwise, get ready for martial law – trust me, it's already being set up, and the number one complicit ally, will be religious leaders. Every great conflict in the history of the world has had the backing of the so called Christian and religious leadership. But the bible speaks of it (check Revelations). It will happen unless black folks act and it's not out of your reach, really, it's not.

First things first. I'm going to start off with saying all of the presidential candidates have something they should be ashamed of when it comes to black America whether it's the 1990 Crime Bill, ignoring criminal justice reform, work as a District Attorney locking up black folks, or not campaigning for black folks the way you want them to campaign for you (Hey Bernie). It's been that way for years, and the only way that will ever change is for folks to vote like Obama is running in every election, National, State, and Local, if they want to be taken seriously, simple- Vote. Vote like it was your grandmother at those lunch counters getting abused. Like it was your mamma who had dogs unleashed on her, or your uncle and brother was attacked by police and illegal/legal mobs and beaten and sprayed with fire hoses; it should be just that personal and straightforward. Now, let's handicap the contenders:

Hillary Clinton – (was still thinking about trying it again) One of the smartest people in any room she walks in. Period. Can she win, probably not. For a couple of reasons, one big one is she seemed to be scared to run on her own accomplishments. Plus, she was to wishy/washy. She called good money when she said half of Trumps supporters were racist (I'm paraphrasing). She was right and she should have stuck to her guns. She didn't get out of pocket until she switched up. Black folks don't like 50/50, can you imagine if she would have come out and said "Yep I said Republicans and I meant it!" Cold gangster, young black folks would have got with that, trust me. Then all of that Bad Girl rhetoric would have resonated and a lot of black girls would have been ride or die for Hillary Clinton! But very intelligent woman, not too many smarter.

Kamal Harris – smart woman, needs more passion. Don't act like she has a lot of skin in the game, could have done more at the Kavanaugh Hearing. Should have went at him like she was prosecuting one of those gangster heavy Hitters in L.A. We know she tough but didn't act like it at the hearing. You were a prosecutor – act like it. Got to the debate and went at Joe, where was that at when Kavanaugh said he blacks out (he said I drink and fall asleep – Dah). Needs to be able to articulate her policies a little better. More seasoning, maybe eight years away.

Corey Booker – smart guy, and he acts like it. He needs to show more of a human side and with passion – showed more when he was mayor of Newark. Would get in the trenches, but too much cautions. Needs to be a little mor authentic, one great moment in the debate (Joe are you high) – needs more of those.

Amy Klobuchar – a smart lady, has heart. Probably too intimidating to a lot of men. She needs to wear it, they are going to call you a battle-ax or ball and chains anyway, so why not wear it. A lot of men (black and white) are intimidated by strong, confident women. But couldn't name world leaders – huh?

Elizabeth Warren – Love her – Personable, a fighter for the working class and the little man. Got plenty of heart, maybe a little too progressive for the country. If she was 10-12 years younger, she would be president one day.

Tom Steyer – Who?? Money can't buy this one.

Pete Buttigieg – Real smart guy, but the country is not ready for an openly gay candidate. Could never get through primaries –

black people are the most homophobic people in the world. If he were straight, he would win in a landslide.

Michael Bloomberg – waited too late to get in – the only candidate to talk real policy – needed more time to get by black people's mistrust but his plan to take back Senate may win him some cool points.

Bernie Sanders – way too progressive, and I mean way too progressive. Plus, he's too old. Young people love him, older people not so much. Bernie, you had a heart attack – come on man. Remember you had a whole network of Hillary Haters rooting you on and helping you along the way. And as quiet as it is kept, Barack did too.

Joe Biden – Smoking Joe. He's old but America loves old White Men! – Always going to have gaffe's – doesn't matter the age. He has had blunders for the last 30 years, so if he has dementia, he has had it since he was 30 – that's Joe. The one thing black folks love about Joe is that he was Obama's ride or die – they feel like they owe him for rolling with Obama, plus, the one thing that separates Smokin Joe from the other's is that he has heart(courage)! You are going to need a lot of heart to clean up this mess.

Now let's move to the Republican side of the Presidential Race. We all know there is only one candidate to really talk about but for arguments sake let's talk about the declared candidates.

Joe Walsh – Tried to make racism fashionable, but just wasn't vulgar and racist enough. Did one thing that most of other Republicans are scared to do, he took on Trump from the beginning and stuck with it. Too bad he was out of office by then.

Gary Johnson – Former Governor of New Mexico. I think he has smoked entirely too much weed. Could hardly name any world leaders on a news program I was watching. space cadet candidate.

William Weld – Former Governor of Massachusetts – Smart guy, won in a Democratic strong hold. But always seems a little spacey to me, nothing to really hang his hat on to say he done anything great. can articulate policy but where he stands, I could never tell you.

Donald Trump – Current President of the United States of America! It really doesn't matter who likes it or not. This is a fact. You will hear black and white people go around and say "Not my President", but guess what, if you are a citizen of the United States of America, he is your President. He won the election, now you may question if it was fair and square? Now that's debatable, sad to say it all depends on who you ask. It shouldn't be but it is. My opinion is that his campaign did cheat, but was it illegal? nope I really don't think it was. I do believe if he could have charged him with a crime Bob Mullear would have. Seemed to be a honest man. It was too much ambiguity at play in the situation. So, he left it to the House of Representative to do the Job. And they dropped the ball. And why? Scared and lazy. But let's move on and look at his why or why he should not be re-elected.

- Presided over one of the largest expansions of the US economy in history
- Record gains in the NY Stock Exchange (over 28,000, S&P +47%)
- Record Tax Cut
- US Troop draw down in Afghanistan and Iraq
- Started Development of the US Space Force

- Jobs Created since he has been President 6.6 million
- Unemployment 3.5%
- Corporate Profits 6%

Now all of these are facts. It cannot be disputed. It's actuality!!! Remember what I said before, "the truth needs know support!" Or as my uncle said "You don't have to like it, but it doesn't stop it from being true. But what we can do is look at the facts. All of this or at least most of it was handed to him. Yep it was, the economy was on a roll and thriving when he took office and I will prove it. Just let's look at the facts:

1) He promised a growth of 4 or 6%, but his average is 2.1. but it was over 2% when he took office and he did nothing to make it rise except the Rich people and Corporate Tax Cut.

2) The Stock market was also thriving when he took office. Let's look at a set of facts. Inauguration day (January 20) 2009. 7,949. Period!

Everybody's 401k was shot! Facts – When Barack Obama left office the stock market was 19,827. So, in other words the stock market rose roughly 150%. So, if Trump stays in office the Dow would have to be 49,369 for him to equal Obama as it relates to the Obama stock market and the Dow Jones industrial Average. Apples to Apples – Obama 12%+ Growth, Trump 8.3% Growth. Simple Facts. And he did not have Banks Failing, Record Home foreclosures and countless other problems that we will not go into, but you get the picture. When black folks hear him talk about a failing economy, most go – Huh? Cuz you tripping, we were here and we saw what was happening. You all have rewrote the record books on slavery but you won't do it on this one, no matter how many Candace Owens and Armstrong Williams you trot out to tell us what we witnessed, we didn't witness!

3) Now about this record tax cut, who benefitted? Not the vast majority of Americans. The average take home pay increased $28 dollars for a bi-weekly paycheck.

But you lost that in your tax refund. Facts! But who did benefit, the top 5% riches Americans and Corporations? Most of the rich folks took their savings from taxes and brought back stocks (70%) in their companies to inflate their financial portfolios, and this was after promising to invest in their company workers and infrastructure. Black folks call that running game. And we say where I'm from Game recognize Game!

4) Troop Draw Down – One thing I don't have a problem with. But I will say this, giving Turkey and Syria that land will come back to bite us in the butt. And turning your back on the Kurds after they did all the heavy lifting in helping us to fight terrorism in that part of the country was real foul.

5) The US Space Force? – Give me a Freaking Brake!!! How about putting that money with the US Pandemic Response Team? (we will talk about that later)

6) Trump 6.6 million Jobs Created, Obama 7.9 Jobs created in the same 35-month period – as we like to say "Say less!"

7) The last 2 can be summed up like this. The unemployment mark is great news, no denying that. But a lot of that was done because of the tax cut, which most economist call a sugar high; Time will tell that story. But Mr. Trump has blown a hole in the deficit. 24%+, somebody will have to pay that money back. All my life I have heard about what great fiscal conservatives' republicans are. I have found that to be one of the biggest lies told under God's creation. They spend on what they want, and you can believe it's not on everyday Americans, George H.W. Bush called it Voodoo Economics and Trickledown Economics before he drank the Kool-Aide.

Now those are a set of facts that cannot be disputed. The thing that always strikes me odd is why more Democrats don't run on these set of facts. If you can't win with these set of facts, you need to get out the game. It's like not being able to win a

Championship with Michael Jordan in his prime! You may have to put in some work and it might get hard but so what! One of the Greatest scenes I have ever seen in a Movie was when Harriet Tubman (The Movie Harriet) said after they had to flee to Canada from Philadelphia after the laws had changed and the slave owners could go in what was considered sanctuary cities (sound familiar) for slaves, And when she was at a meeting and she had informed the other freed slaves and Abolitionist that she was going back to get more slaves and bring them to freedom. Most looked at her like she was crazy, her response "You think I'm gonna stop because it's far?" – Now that's a real G right there! Any time I need inspiration for something I am doing I watch that scene, that one scene spoke volumes to me and it should to every American, Black or White. I remember when the fight for healthcare seemed to be fading and Barack held a press conference and told the press as critics tried to punch holes in his ideals for the new law. He told them "We are Americans!!! "my uncle used to say the same thing about different situations, yeah its hard but that's all that means is just that, it doesn't mean we don't do it, it just means that it's hard, but so are we!

HOUSE OF REPRESENITIVES

Now, I will only say one thing about the House, thank God for Nancy Pelosi. If the United States didn't have Nancy Pelosi, they would be in big trouble. I am always taken aback why no other men seems to have the heart Nancy Pelosi, and Maxine Waters have. They hand Mr. Trump his lunch and dinner whenever given the chance.

Real American Heroes' in my book.
The Senate – please go to www.Vote.gov.

Check Schumer – should be arrested for crimes against humanity – how in God's Name could you strike a deal with Mitch McConnell. For such a deal allowing a straight vote to put such a large number of incompetent judges on the Federal Bench – you should be arrested, a disgrace!

Now there should be some seats in the Senate that's flipped and here the most likely candidates:

Florida – register to vote www.Florida.gov
North Carolina – www.NCSBE.gov

Ohio – www.Ohiosos.gov

Texas – yep Texas – www.voteTexas.gov

Wisconsin – www.Wisconsin.gov>myvote

Colorado – www.colorado.gov

Arizona – www.azsos.gov

Pennsylvania – www.pa.gov

AND

Kentucky – I saved this for last – How can you keep electing this grifter to congress – He keeps coal mines open to kill all of you – not renewable energy but coal. It's killing you, facts: the carbon dioxide is killing you. You can put a renewable energy program in place of the coal mines and live. WOW – he needs to go. How can you say your number one goal is to make somebody a one term president regardless of how much that person tries to help all Americans? He still has to go? I hope not only Louisville and Lexington come out to vote him out, but Radcliff and Shively also; all in all, his policies don't just hurt black people but all Kentuckians. When you go to the hospital, they don't check your melanin, they check to see how much carbon is in your lungs.

Let's just look at Glasgow's poverty rate 26.9%. with a average household income is $30,000. $30,000, that's right I said it twice so you can understand it. $30,000 a household, not per person. FBI Crime data says it is not one of the safest places to live. It has a crime rate that is higher than 90% of the cities and towns of the state, check it. Go to neighborhood scout. Facts, check FBI Data, guess what 84% white, 8% Black, 5% Latino – seems to me that Moscow Mitch and Mr. Rand Paul should be doing whatever they can to make these people lives better. Instead of making somebody a one term president. Help the people of Glasgow. Kentucky has 10 of the poorest counties in the whole country. take a look at Floyd County, Jackson County, Martin County and Knox County. All with a poverty level over 20%. The people of these places need you more than Obama did and definitely more than Donald Trump. Now, like I said, this is the truth. You don't have to like it, but guess what, it doesn't stop it from being true. Now last think on this subject. Let's look at the ten poorest states in America and their US Senators - Facts:

Mississippi Poverty Rate 19%:
2 Republicans Senators, (R) Cindy Smith/(R) Roger Wicker

New Mexico, Poverty Rate 19.5%:

(D) Tom Udall/(D) Martin Heinrich

Louisiana: Poverty Rate 18.6%

Two Republican Senators (R) Bill Cassidy/John Kennedy,

West Virginia: Poverty Rate 17.8%

One Democrat/One Republican, (R) Shelley Moore/(D) John Manchin

Alabama – Poverty Rate 16.6%

One Democrat, One Republican/(D) Doug Jones, (R) Richard Shelby

Kentucky – Poverty Rate 16.9%

Two Republicans Mitch McConnell/Rand Paul

South Carolina – Poverty Rate 15%

Two Republicans (R) Lindsay Graham/(R) Tim Scott

Arkansas – Poverty Rate 17.2%

(R) John Boozman / (R) Tom Cotton

Tennessee – Poverty Rate 15%

Two Republicans (R) Lamar Alexander/(R) Marsha Blackburn

Oklahoma – Poverty Rate 15.6%

(R) James Langford/ (R) James Inhofe

This is all factual, Americans and most citizens for these great states should be demanding Town Halls so you can ask them why your states are so poor, why if I work at least 40 hours a week do I still need to get food stamps and then if I work and do need help, why are you cutting food stamp programs. Simple. Hold them accountable.

Democrats, Republicans, Independent, Jew, Gentile, it doesn't matter. Remember, with all the damage Mr. Trump has done to this country. He has had help daily. Remember, no matter how wrong Trump is, he cannot destroy this country alone, he needs help. Hitler didn't bring Germany to its knees all by himself. He had a lot of help. And something a lot of people don't want to admit, but a lot of Jewish help, especially in the beginning. If you look at all the other notorious criminals in this country's history such as Al Capone (Frank Nitti), John Dillinger (Pretty Boy Floyd and others), Jesse James (Younger Brothers, Frank James), John Gotti (Sammy the Bull), they all had help, and Mr. Trump has had plenty. Now, let me be clear until Mr. Trump put into place his extortion plot in Ukraine, he hadn't committed a crime. I think his son did, but that's just speculation. He may be the most unethical and immoral man ever to hold the office of President (Andrew Jackson was a murderer, and we have him on a 10-dollar bill). Until Ukraine, he hadn't done anything criminal that anybody could prove. Do I think he sold this country out to Russia and Saudi Arabia? Yep! But, that's pure speculation! Do I think Russia has some of our most sensitive secrets and could put this country in harms' way for years to come?

Yes, I do, but that's my opinion. Do I think his kids are using the country to make deals and steal? Yep, but that's innuendo, no real proof. Do I believe he is robbing this country with all of these golfing trips, and we, the taxpayers, are footing the bill? Yep. Is it illegal? Nope. Unethical? Yep. Illegal? Nope. Did he and his family steal from a cancer charity? Yep, (facts) before he was President. Is it illegal? Yep, he settled on this. Did he defraud thousands at his fraudulent University (facts)? Yep! Before he was President, he settled, and millions had to be repaid. He still made millions because only some was returned.

Do I think he is a coward and comes from a generation of cowards (his sons following in the same footsteps)? Yep, I do. I may be embellishing a bit on this part of the story. Rumor has it that his daddy and granddaddy left Germany because they didn't want to defend their country. So, I may have embellished a little. Do I think his mom and dad was a part of the Klan? Maybe. I've seen the pictures with his mom in Klan a outfit. Black folk's news flash, that was doctored. It's not real, somebody photo shop it. But we do know his farther was arrested at a Klan rally in New York in 1927. He denies it but it's a record of it.

Do I think he's a billionaire, absolutely not? You may assess his properties, but he won't show his taxes so it can only be assessed on what he owns or does not own. I don't know any narcissists who are not willing to brag whenever they can. Still, that is just conjecture and speculation. Until Ukraine alleged extortion crime, he hadn't done anything criminal that could be proven.

He may be unethical, incompetent, ignorant, and a liar, but until Ukraine, he was just that, and that's not criminal. They only way to fix this is to vote and not just this one coming up in 2020, but all elections when you have time.

Please look at this video:

https//www.youtube.com/watch?v=wMaler1-FM, the guys' name is Yellow Pain. He breaks it all the way down. Please watch and as I close, one last thing, for all you people of color hitching your wagon to the Trump train, just a little insight: Did you know that while Hitler was killing Jews all over Europe, it was still Jews walking around in Germany as free men without fear of persecution until they couldn't. So, while he wage's war on people of color and talked about Obama, just remember your time will come. When he talks about Obama, he sees every black child in the same light. Whenever he sees Hispanic judges in a negative light, he sees the young Latino who strives to be that judge. But then again, it's all just speculation.
Extra:

Now some observations from the Author:

As I close, but not ending this book, there are a couple of things I want to make explicitly clear. There is one thing that I will not do, and I will not ever do, and that is lie. I just will not do it, at least not intentionally! I may wish that Donald Trump's Presidency will end after one term, that's not an intentional lie if it doesn't happen, that was just speculation that happens to be wrong. Second, I will not participate in fake news, nor will I condone it or promote it. I will not look for reasons to give anyone a pass, Republicans or Democrats, nope not happening. I watched a debate and saw 2 or 3 Democrat candidates struggle with naming world leaders – that's a disgrace. The DNC Head should have walked on the stage and dismissed them right there. It's like Republicans presented a dumb man and the Democrats say I will see you two (Klobuchar and Steyer), I mean for real.

I mean, you want to lead the free world and don't know the name of the President of Mexico. I wanted to ask them to name the three branches of the Government. The Republicans send an old white man, the Democrats say I got 4 (Steyer, Biden, Bernie and Bloomberg). Come on guys you need energy, and most of the time, that's somebody young and innovative, energetic and hungry to make a difference.

THE BLACK WOMAN VOTE

I would like to thank the black women personally for keeping the alleged pedophile out of the Senate. Y'all did it even after Mr. Trump endorsed (you know the creep who fantasizes about dating his daughter) him. You all came from Birmingham, Montgomery, Huntsville, and others places and brought it to the table. Now just think if the black men had responded in kind between 60 to 75% of African Americans make up the population in these two cities of Alabama (Montgomery and Birmingham). That's over 60% close to 70% of 400,000. You do the math. If you vote (black men), you can say who goes where, period, and the strong thing about it, for the most part, black and white people want the same things. Everybody wants good schools, good health care, decent jobs, low crime. Politics have separated us, and it's the politicians who have created this. Same thing in Mississippi- the cities of Jackson, Shelby, and Greenville make ups over 70% of African American people. How do you all keep electing incompetent people to represent you? Why don't you vote? I don't care under what party affiliation; you have 2 million people in Mississippi and close to 40% of that is African Americans, black folks.

Everybody wants the same thing, black and white, and this is one of the poorest states in the country. Crazy right – I think so!

BLACK MEN

Come on, black men, it's time to lead. Get out there and become president and neighborhood captains and make sure people are registered to vote and then vote – simple. IT can be done. Go to www.vote.org or www.vote.gov or Google and find out who the contact person is in your party affiliation and start there. Set up a Town Hall meeting, or voter registration drive. Ask the party leaders for help and then see what happens. Dollars to doughnuts that they will get all in. Some of the people I mentioned in previous chapters have no right to collect a government check or receive the kind of healthcare that they deny you.

I remember when Ted Cruz was running for President and said that he had to accept Obama Care because of his family. Did he vote to deny other families the same opportunities, and millions of people still voted for that hypocrite, crazy, right? Easy fix. Whatever healthcare policy that Congress votes on, that's what he receives.

If you vote no for affordable healthcare, you shouldn't get it period. Make it an individual approach. They all should be drug tested, from the President to every member of Congress and Judges. The bottom line is America needs the black men to step up.

COVID-19

Now at the time of the publishing of this book, the Covid-19 was beginning to ravish this country in a terrifying way. It's a lot that has been already said about this horrific virus so I will not go into a lot about what some of the obvious things that has happened. But I will attempt to enlighten some on just a few things.

- ❖ The entire Trump Administration should be arrested for Negligent Homicide. They watched and just waited while this virus came here and exploded on the scene and done nothing with a great big assist from Fox News. Now they are trying to rewrite the record books. I have seen them get on TV and watch them spin it like over 40,000 deaths is not that bad. WOW!!! And the Leader of China is supposed to be his boy. Oh really, it's a whole lot that's wrong with this picture. A whole lot, but congress will not get down to the bottom of it because the Trump Administration will stonewall and not release the records on what really happened. But it's one or two things, pure incompetence or total negligence. One or the other. And the Lies and the rewriting of history has already started.

❖ Somebody help me with this one, a Pandemic Response Team built just for situation like this. And this is just intuitive, the team was supposed to locate a potential problem all over the world and then dispatch to that region of the world and start battling the problem there, not wait for it to get to America and then begin the fight. But stop me if I said something that wasn't right. So, if Mr. Trump and John Bolton fired, dismantled or disband this department. What should this be called. Now everybody all over the world was saying something like this was going to happen, so Obama successfully stopped the spread of Ebola and saw that something like this would be beneficial to not only America but the world. But nope, it had the Obama name on it (speculation) so we don't need it. I will say this if nobody else will, after all the death and sickness is said and done the blood of these people are on the hands of Donald Trump, John Bolton and every other National Security Expert that was on the watch!!!!!!! YOU FAILED AND IT COST AMERICAN LIVES!!!! TRUTH AND FACTS!

❖ This Virus has exposed the so-called invincibility of who we Americans think we are. Black folks and white folks alike. In the black community we heard over and over again that this disease could not affect black folks. And now what, we have become science deniers just like the Trump Clan. What happen was the Perfect Horrific Storm. COVID-19! Why for Black Folks – Let's look at a set of facts, lack of exercise, poor diet and eating habits lead to health problems (Diabetes, High Blood Pressure, Heart Disease). Essential Workers (Fireman, Police, Correctional and Security Officers, Postal Workers, Public Transportation Drivers and Operators, Sanitation Workers) – a vast number of these positions are filled by black and brown people, especially in major and urban cities. Access to affordable healthcare. And last but not least "Black People can't get this Virus- we got strong genes!" (Same thing I heard when Aids First Hit). And don't forget FBI has warned that white extremist and supremacy groups was discussing ways on how to spread the virus to police, Jewish and people of color. (check ABC News and the FBI New York field Office) So what's the results, close to 40% of all deaths are from people of color.

LAST BUT NOT LEAST – EMPATHY

This is the most lacking characteristic missing in society as a whole. It's not even close, and the leaders of this madness start with the so-called Faith Leaders, Pastors, Men of the Cloth, Clergy, and Preachers. I don't care what you call them, if you would like to challenge me on this, I welcome it.

Remember the one thing Jesus told His Disciples, "By this will people know that you are one of mine by the love you have one to another!" He told His disciples, I was hungry, and you didn't feed me, I was naked, and you didn't clothe me – their response, Master when did we see you like this? His response, when you see the least in my Kingdom.

The lack of empathy won't let you look beyond yourself and give out a little helping hand. One day I was doing some ridesharing, and I gave some money to a homeless guy looking for something in the trash can to eat. My passenger, who I had just been talking to about the goodness of the Lord, asked me, how do you know he won't buy drugs and alcohol with it?

I'm supposed to judge a man who is eating out of a trash can, but be okay knowing they filled a wagon up with money and gave it to her Pastor to go on vacation. Something is wrong with this picture. I mean crazy, right? There is no empathy from so-called Christian's running rampant, and we ask ourselves why millennials are turning away from God. Start at the head; church leaders are supposed to lead. If some of these megachurch pastors were to show some empathy instead of asking for money for a new jet or new car, or a new sanctuary and attempt to eradicate hunger and homelessness in their city, the world would be a better place. Perhaps they should say things like, "We are going to build the largest food pantry and kitchen this city has ever seen" or, "We are going to build the largest homeless shelter with a healthcare facility that people have ever seen." How do you think the congregation would react? How do you think the people of that city would we react? How would the politicians react? It's the Pastors' words and actions that people follow – I know it is said we should follow Christ, and I do, but we all look to the angel of the church for directions.

During the great Civil Rights Movement, it was true men of God that led that movement. They were not like the men who visit with Mr. Trump, while he asks you about your congregation size, and you pray for him, and he looks at you like you are crazy. In case anyone wants to know, prayer is a time of humility, just to keep it real, if you are going to God and you are not humble, I don't care who you are, you need a lesson in basic biblical principles. I do want people to know I am a believer. I do believe in Christ and Him crucified. I believe He died for my sins, I believe in Heaven, and I believe in Hell. I do think I have to love in order to see Jesus face. Now you may say what does that have to do with Donald Trump? Just so knows I have no choice but to love Mr. Trump if I want to make it to Heaven, period. I don't like his ways and what he does, but I have to find a way to love him and pray for him. This is why what Nancy Pelosi said resonated so much with all true believers, and not with religious (Pharisees) people. They only want to love those who love them. Black people have to love Donald Trump and pray for him. The Bible says that much, now that's the truth!!

THE BIG FINISH, SO LET'S SUMMARIZE:

- The number one problem facing this country from my point of view is Empathy. I have watched President after President display compassion, empathy and sensitivity to the people of America for as long as I have been living, UNTIL NOW!!! This President does not seem to have an understanding of how that works. He seems to be void of any real understanding or feelings for his fellow man. It doesn't matter if they are from Europe, The United States of American or his next-door neighbor. It really doesn't matter to him. His lack of empathy would be okay if it was just him in this world, but he has a whole country to care about, and 300 million people is too much to be void of that emotion. Truth be told I think it may be too much responsibility for him to handle. Another problem with this type of behavior is that it has rubbed off on a lot of other Americans. I'm not just talking about racist people, but every day tried and true Americans have slipped into this merciless mindset. Even in the Black Community, I have heard black folks say they should treat these white people that are suffering from opioid addiction the same way they treated black people that suffered from the crack epidemic. I think that is wrong, and for a so-called Christian to say it is double wrong. Black folks have been able to come from where they come from because of their sense of community and their amazing ability to have empathy. They way black folks were treated doing the Crack epidemic was wrong, real wrong. It's a whole laundry list of ways the Black community was treated doing these times, but the black community is bigger than hoping someone else goes thru the same thing you did for the sake of so-called fairness. Remember, everyone is, "somebody's someone!" Love and Compassion is who the Black community is, this is why we fill churches up on Sunday Mornings. At least that's what your mouth says! Jesus said, "Be Ye Not Hearers but Doers of the Word!" So, you say you love everybody, start loving them and stop judging them so much.

- Why should the Black community love Mr. Trump? Because the bible tells us so. It's just that simple. Jesus said, (here I go again) "Love your enemy and love those who despitefully use you!" Also, you have to pray for him. Check 1 Timothy 2:1-4. We need to be praying for the entire government but him especially. I know it's hard, but it's true. I always say if you are not going to try to do what the Bible says you probably should stop going to church and save that money. That's just an opinion.

- Last, but not least, when you look at all the things that Mr. Trump has done you may ask yourself WHY??? If it wasn't for Mr. Trump How much would you really be grateful for. I watched after Barack Obama's Historic win and how a lot of Black folks forgot about the struggle that got us to that point. Now Black folks have begun to reflect again about the struggle and all the sacrifice that was made for them. They can now see that it wasn't as easy as they would like to believe. Nope, it wasn't easy at all. It makes you just that much more grateful, sort of like this journey of life and having Jesus as your Lord and Savior. If you did not have the devil on your trail so much, would you really pray as hard as you do, if he wouldn't try to steal your seed (finances, family, mental and emotional well-being) would you look to God for direction and fast the way that you do? Would you depend on his understanding as much or would you just lean on your own for the most part? Yeah, I think you get the picture!

My prayer is that you would receive this book as a tool of enlightenment and allow it to inspire you to stay woke and continue to fight (not physical but through voting and dialogue) for the America that Dr, King envisioned for your kids as well as mine. Always remember the truth will never need support. In closing, I leave you with what my Uncle use to always tell me – "Jonathan, you don't have to like the truth, but that doesn't stop it from being true."

GRACE and PEACE, and Thank You for the Support.

Just as reminder, some other great information for the love fest we have for Mr. Trump come November. And some of the other candidates who choose to become a part of the Problem and not the solution.

Check voter status – www.voteamerica.com

STATE AND LOCAL ELECTION BOARDS:

Georgia – www.Georiga.Gov – (18yrs) use the MVP tool to check your status

Louisiana – www.Louisiana.Gov – (17yrs) use the online voter tool – use the search menu- 30 days prior to election to vote

Mississippi – www.msvoterid.gov – (18yrs)) request voter Id form – 30 days prior to election to vote

Alabama – www.Alabama.Gov – (18yrs) request postcard voter registration card – 14 days prior to election – can register at all local and state offices

Kentucky – www.Ky.gov – (18yrs) Request form for registration -30 days prior to election to register

North Carolina – www.ncdot.com – (18yrs) Can Register online – 30 days prior to election

South Carolina – www.SCVote.org – (18yrs) Online registration – 30 days prior to election

Pennsylvania – www.PA.gov – (18yrs) Website application submission ok. - 30 days prior to election

Michigan - www.mvic.sos.state.us –(18yrs) Online Registration ok – 30 days prior to election

Wisconsin – www.votewisconsin.com – (18yrs) Online Registration ok – 30 prior to election

Republican National Committee – www.GOP.Com

Democratic National Committee- www.democrats.org

Now folks please use this information. Your life and your love one's life depend on it. Use the information and call for a absentee ballot right now. Host a town hall meeting, call the respective political parties and tell them you want to host a town hall. it's a lot simpler than you think. But the most important thing to do now is to start now.

Step #1 - Get your ID – you need it anyway.

Step #2 - Register to Vote – you and your family depends on it

Step #3 – Request an Absentee Ballot – they will send it to you

Step #4 - Look at the Yellow Pain Video on YouTube My Vote Counts

Step #5 – **ENGAGE** *– Your life depends on it*
Covid-19 - 90,000 lives and counting
35 million jobs lost
National Debt- 23.3 Trillion
Hate Crimes at 16-year High
Over 135 School shootings in last 3 years

Your life really do depend on it !!!

ABOUT THE AUTHOR

Johnny (Big) Dawgs was born and raised in Washington, DC, during the exciting times of the 1960s and the 70s. When he graduated in 1978 from Annapolis High School, he had enough first-hand experience that inspired him to write about the black narrative that is currently happening in this country.

After becoming an adult, he questioned his religious upbringing and became a willing participant in the underground street culture. One day while following his wife to church, he happened to hear a man preaching. The man's words reignited something in his soul. The sermon touched his heart and inspired him to rededicate his life to Christ. His upbringing gave him a keen understanding on how the church is run and operated. Big Dawg saw the birth of the so-called megachurch in the 1990s.

Banking on his versatility, experience, and knowledge on knowing how to read his audience, Dawgs can tailor his message to anyone, be it a layman, a street man, a spiritual man, or a businessman. His ability and love for people allowed him to reach both the common man and the businessman and inspired him to become a Certified Life Coach.

Big Dawgs is not alone on his life journey. He has been married for more than 30 years, and they have two adult children and one Grandson together. He also has two surrogate brothers and four surrogate sisters who share in his accomplishments.

Jonathon's favorite saying is, "My life experiences shape my opinion. Facts are based on Data, and my feelings back my opinions."

www.ingramcontent.com/pod-product-compliance
Lightning Source LLC
Chambersburg PA
CBHW022116090426
42743CB00008B/879